A GUIDE THROUGH LENT

TO WALK WITH JESUS

ROBERTA PARKER MARTIN

AVE MARIA PRESS
Notre Dame, Indiana 46556

ROBERTA PARKER MARTIN is a retreat leader and licensed counselor, as well as the volunteer director of Wellspring, a non-profit organization promoting Christian growth and retreat ministry. She earned her doctorate in ministry from Columbia Theological Seminary and was ordained a Presbyterian minister in 1987. Although she has written a number of journal articles, *To Walk With Jesus* is her first book.

Excerpts are taken from the NEW REVISED STANDARD VERSION, copyright © 1991 by Oxford University Press, Inc. Reprinted by permission of the publisher.

Noted excerpts are from THE NEW JERUSALEM BIBLE, copyright © 1985 by Darton, Longman & Todd, Ltd. and Doubleday & Company, Inc. Reprinted by permission of the publisher.

International Standard Book Number: 0-87793-520-3

Library of Congress Catalog Card Number: 93-74039

Cover and text design by Elizabeth J. French

Photography: Bob and Miriam Francis cover; Vernon Sigl 17, 120-121; Justin A. Soleta 28-29, 44-45, 62-63, 82-83, 102-103.

Printed and bound in the United States of America.

Acknowledgments

As I ponder the ones I want to thank, a parade of people ambles through my memory, all companions in some way on my spiritual journey. The ones who have touched my life, helping me to see more clearly and feel more deeply, are somehow reflected in these pages even though they go unnamed.

But there are some that I must name who in a direct way touched the manuscript. Special thanks to each of the following:

—to Rev. O. Wendell Manual who asked me to write a "brief description of Lent" for members of his congregation; his request served as the impetus to begin writing, which already felt like a sacred call; my "description" is now part of the introduction, but for me, my response to the call was not complete until the last meditation was finished.

—to Barbara, Jeannette, Sarah, and Rose who gave faithful prayer support during the birthing process and to the members of the Lenten study group at Trinity Presbyterian Church, Starkville, Mississippi, who used these meditations weekly as they came out of my computer—Barbara McKee, Tom and Kitty Jones, Warren and Judy Housley, Bob and Jan Taylor, Liz Stiffler, Helen Sue Parrish, Rose Finley, and especially Ginger Jones who pulled me aside after the second week of Lent and said earnestly, "You must get these published for others";

—to Kay Verrall, a companion of the soul, who used the meditations during Lent and whose candor and eagle eye eliminated many of the original blemishes;

—to Etta Wilson, president of March Media, Nashville, Tennessee, a special friend and spiritual companion of many, many years who read the completed manuscript and believed in it, and in me, just when I needed it most;

—to Frank Cunningham of Ave Maria Press who received the manuscript enthusiastically, a special gift to a new author, and to Peggy Parente Ehling who gently smoothed out the rough edges and confirmed my gratitude that the manuscript was in the capable hands of Ave Maria;

—to Curtis and Andrew, our sons, who graciously put up with me throughout the writing and, finally, especially to Ed, my life companion who proofed and cheered, and proofed and proofed and still cheered some more, and proofed and prodded and cheered again! How did God know how much I would need an over-zealous cheerleader to complete this task?!

For each of these I say a heartfelt "thanks be to God!"

Contents

Meditations for the Forty Days of Lent

Introduction: Tools for the Journey

In the very early church, part of the Easter celebration was the baptism of new converts and the renewal of the baptismal vows by those who were already Christian. In preparation for these events, there was a time of fasting and repentance. This time of preparation is the origin of our present day Lenten season.

Some of us have grown up within Christian traditions that still celebrate the season of Lent beginning with an Ash Wednesday service and culminating in the baptismal celebration at the Easter Vigil. Some of us have grown up within traditions that mention the season of Lent, change the pulpit cloths to purple, and do little else. Some of us have grown up within traditions that make no mention of Lent at all. If you have picked up this book, you are probably in the group of people who want to know more about the season of Lent and how to observe it.

Lent consists of the forty days preceding Easter Sunday, beginning with Ash Wednesday and not counting the Sundays. It is a time of preparation for the Easter celebration. Part of the Lenten focus is on Jesus' journey to Jerusalem and on the events that preceded Jesus' death and resurrection. In Romans 6, Paul tells us that if we die with Christ, we shall surely rise with him. Therefore, part of the Lenten focus is an examination of our own lives to determine those parts of us that need to die, or those parts of us that we need to let go (old habits, grudges, resentments, fears, etc.), so that we too may experience resurrection even now. Lent is about Jesus' journey to Jerusalem and about our journey to Jerusalem with him.

In Mark's gospel Jesus says to his weary disciples, "Come away to a deserted place all by yourselves and rest a while" (Mark 6:31). Jesus invites us to do the same—to come rest a while with him, to come apart and know him better. His invitation to his disciples can be our Lenten invitation. But how do we do that? The following suggestions are offered to help you get started on this Lenten journey.

Place and Time: Set aside a special place for your Lenten meditations if you do not already have such a place. Gather your Bible, a notebook, a pen, this book, and any other devotional material you might plan to use and put them in your designated place. The only requirement for the space is that it be a place comfortable to you and as free from distractions as possible. Sometimes it helps to have a special symbol that is meaningful to you in this place. Items such as a candle (a reminder that Christ has come to be a light in all of our dark places, or Christ as the light of the world has also called us to be a light in the world), a flower or bulb (a reminder that after the darkest winter, spring will come again), or a rock (a symbol of the unchanging, faithfulness of God) are possibilities. Any symbol may be used that is meaningful to you in your quest for greater intimacy with God, but no symbol is necessary.

Any time that works for you is the right time. Setting a special time and keeping that time as you would an appointment with the most important person in your life works for many people and is often recommended. Early morning, noon time, or late evening can all work depending on the rhythm of your own life. Jesus prayed at all times of day and night.

Part of creating space and time for God is to carve out that space within. An attitude of expectancy and openness to God's Spirit can make any place and any time the right time and place for prayer.

Prayer and Quiet Time: Prayer is a two-way conversation. Too often we spend our prayer time doing all the talking. In 1732 Thomas Fuller wrote, "'Tis easier to know how to speak than how to be silent." His words are still true. In our fast paced, noisy world it is often hard to become still inside. If you have trouble becoming quiet, are bothered by lists of things to do or extraneous thoughts that keep creeping in, it sometimes helps to stop and write down the list just to get it out of the way. Try beginning your quiet time by simply asking for God's special presence. Give yourself time to be still. Practice being in the presence of God—it does take practice. Breathe deeply, gently, slowly, letting the tensions and outer thoughts drain from your mind.

Some find it helpful to use a "prayer word" or "prayer phrase" for focus. Words like holy, peace, love, hope, or words of the Trinity, God, Jesus, Spirit, or phrases such as "God's love," "peace of God," or "come Spirit" are sometimes used. When extraneous thoughts come, refocusing on the word or phrase can bring you back to center. Such words do not always form a prayer, but can be a gentle reminder to help us focus.

If you have trouble praying or saying to God what you want to say, try writing it down like you were writing to a friend (see suggestions for keeping a journal below). Jesus called us his friends and wants us to be comfortable with him and to talk with him in whatever way is easiest for us.

Author James Finley tells the following story about his own struggle with prayer.

> Merton once told me to quit trying so hard in prayer. He said: "How does an apple ripen? It just sits in the sun." A small green apple cannot ripen in one night by tightening all its muscles, squinting its eyes, and tightening its jaw in order to find itself the next morning miraculously large, red, ripe, and juicy beside its small green counterparts. Like the birth of a baby or the opening of a rose, the birth of the true self takes place in God's time. We must wait for God, we must be awake; we must trust in his hidden action within us (*Merton's Palace of Nowhere*).

Keeping a Journal: It's very helpful to take notes or to write responses to the meditation questions. If you already keep a journal, you can plan to use it in conjunction with the book. However, if you choose not to write your responses, it will be helpful at the end of each week to reflect on where your journey has taken you.

If you have never kept a journal this may be a good time to give it a try. Any kind of notebook will do. A spiral notebook or any notebook with blank pages will work. Loose pages can be easily lost, but if that is all you have available, use what you have. Date all entries. This will be meaningful to you as you read back through what you have written later. Journals can be used in a variety of ways. They are often used for recording prayers, meaningful moments, passages of scripture, new insights, hopes, plans for the future, dreams, happenings, ideas, goal setting, or dialogues with scripture.

Scripture: The Bible is a book that is still fresh and alive today, not just a collection of ancient recordings. However, sometimes it is difficult to know how to find that freshness. One thing that is sometimes helpful is remembering that everything Jesus said to his disciples long ago he says to his disciples now. The setting may be different, but the meaning is the same. The letters of Paul and Peter, once written to churches long ago, are still letters written to churches today, to us. Prophets spoke to people in exile, to people worshipping false gods, to people loved by God, and so on; those same prophets still speak to those of us caught in our own exiles, still worshipping false gods, and still loved by God!

The Lenten season is a good time to read one of the gospels from beginning to end. Ask for God's special presence as you begin. Read it not sentence by sentence or verse by verse, but section by section or chapter by chapter as you would any other book. Imagine yourself in the passage. How would you have felt, responded, acted if you had been there? How do you respond now?

Dialoguing with scripture takes the above suggestions a little further. Dialoguing with scripture also requires more time. To dialogue with scripture, select a passage that seems to speak to you. Read the passage reflectively several times. Identify with one of the people in the passage. Enter into the situation through the person with whom you identify. To do this, first relax. Close your eyes. Picture the person with whom you identify. View the whole situation through this person's eyes.

Write your perceptions in your journal. Write in the first person—"I ...." Be sure to write all the perceptions that come to you. Include situation, place, feelings, reactions, images, and requests. Set your imagination free to explore tangents to the narrative. Let it take you where it will.

After writing a description of the events you have seen, felt, heard, etc., engage Jesus in a dialogue. Ask him whatever questions come to you. Then write his response. Keep the dialogue going until it is finished.

After writing, sit quietly. Be with the experience. Re-experience the wholeness of this encounter. Read what you have written. Ponder the images, feelings, perceptions, and ideas that came to you. Feel the message in its wholeness. What has been said to you by the Spirit? What of God has been revealed?

In response to this total experience, write a prayer that expresses your deepest understanding of who you are as you sit in the presence of God.

When we pray, we are able to bring the scriptures to life in our hearts. Praying scripture is simply what it says it is—praying scripture, or praying the prayers of scripture, or praying through an especially meaningful event of scripture. Let the words become your own or guide your own. The psalms particularly lend themselves to this kind of prayer.

Spiritual Directors: Just as it is sometimes more fun and more rewarding to take a trip with a friend, so it is in traveling the spiritual journey. It can be helpful to have a spiritual director or spiritual companion who will journey with you.

Choose a person you respect who feels called to walk with you on this journey. A spiritual director, companion, or friend is usually a person who is spiritually mature, aware of his or her own spiritual journey, knowledgeable of scripture and the Christian faith. The person you choose should be a person who is a good listener and who is accepting of you, no matter how mature or immature you are at the moment and regardless of your successes or failures. Honesty and dependability are important qualities, as is confidentiality.

Your spiritual director or companion will act as a source of support and encouragement during your journey. Set up several regular meetings during the time you are working through this book—maybe even weekly meetings. The person should be able to really listen to you as you share whatever has surfaced as you work through the exercises. It is important that you feel free to share whatever you need to about your life—your insights, your questions, your fears, the hard places, the surprises. Your director may raise questions for you, make suggestions from his or her understanding of scripture, faith, or the spiritual journey. The director's function is to help you understand what God is doing in your life; the emphasis is on your journey as it unfolds. Ask the person to pray with you and for you as you open yourself to a new understanding of yourself and a deeper relationship with God.

Small Prayer Groups: For many people, the support of a group of friends traveling together can be essential on the journey. You may want to start meeting with a small group of companions during this Lenten journey. This could be done as part of a regular parish or church education program during Lent or just as a weekly gathering of friends in someone's home. Usually a group size of twelve or under works well for this kind of study. If the group is larger than twelve, you might want to consider breaking into two groups. Some of the following group guidelines may be helpful.

1.   Decide on a place and time of meeting. If used during a regular parish program, the time frame is already set. If you are meeting in a home, decide on a beginning and ending time (usually not more than two hours) and stick to it. Socializing time could be before or after.

2.   A leader should be designated for the first session or all the sessions. Leadership could be passed around. The role of the leader is to begin and end the meeting and see that opportunity for sharing is given to all. The preparation for the leader is the same as for each participant—openness to God's presence and commitment to working through each of the daily meditations.

3.   It is helpful to establish some guidelines for the group from the beginning such as confidentiality, not judging another's experience, freedom to "pass" when the group is sharing, and so on. The guidelines work best when the group establishes them. You could begin with a question like, "What helps you feel safe in a group?" Let the list of guidelines form as the participants share what safe means for them.

4.   Begin each session with a prayer of thanksgiving for God's promised presence wherever two or three are

gathered, and a prayer for openness to the experience of God's presence.

5. Begin the sessions by giving each person a *brief* chance to say which of the meditations were most meaningful, least meaningful, or most difficult. The person might also indicate if there was a particular meditation they would like to discuss with the group. This will give each person in the group a chance to participate if desired and will give the leader and the group a chance to see how the rest of the time should be divided.

6. Provide every member of the group with a list of the names of the other group members, so that each person may pray for the other members during the week. Suggest that the group members commit to praying for each other daily.

7. Always end the group with prayer for any of the concerns and struggles that may have surfaced during the time together. Joining hands as you pray is meaningful for many, but be sensitive to the needs of the group. The leader might lead the closing prayer during the first weeks if the group is not already comfortable together. As the group becomes more comfortable with each other, the closing time might be a time of silence in which members pray as they feel led, possibly closing with the Lord's Prayer.

To Walk With Jesus uses many of the tools mentioned above to help you focus your Lenten journey. Even if you begin after Ash Wednesday, begin working with *To*

Walk With Jesus with the Ash Wednesday meditation and proceed from there since one meditation often builds on another, especially in the beginning. May God's presence surround you as you walk this Lenten journey and may you experience a new glimpse of resurrection.

Roberta Parker Martin

Meditations
for the
Forty Days
of Lent

Ash Wednesday

"Before I formed you in the womb I knew you, and before you were born I consecrated you ...."
—Jeremiah 1:5

The LORD is near to all who call on him, to all who call on him in truth.
—Psalm 145:18

[Jesus] said to them, "Come away to a deserted place all by yourselves and rest a while."
—Mark 6:31

Lent cannot be separated from Easter, for Lent is a time of returning, of coming home to a God who loves us more than we can imagine—no matter how we come or how long we have been away. Lent is a time of coming home to all that God created us to be—a time to die to the old or let go of those things that hold us back in order to be raised to new life. Lent is a time of letting go of the old bondage that we might experience resurrection.

The whole of Jesus' journey to Jerusalem, to the cross and to resurrection, was to show us how much he loves us. To make a pilgrimage through Lent is to take a spiritual journey. We are on that journey in one way or another for most of our lives. Sometimes we are in deserts and sometimes on mountaintops. But to journey through Lent is to take an intentional journey to resurrection. We must come just as we are. The only way we can begin any journey is to start from where we are; there is no other place to begin.

Stop now and write a paragraph or two completing this sentence: "This is a time in my life when ...." Be as specific and honest as you can.

Prayer Suggestion:

Read back over the paragraph you have just written and offer who you are and where you are at this time in your life to God. This is where you are as you begin your Lenten journey. Ask for God's presence even now and as you walk the rest of the journey. Make notes of anything else that comes to you during your prayer time.

Thursday after Ash Wednesday

Now when Jesus came into the district of Caesarea
Philippi, he asked his disciples, "Who do people say
that the Son of Man is?" And they said, "Some say
John the Baptist, but others Elijah, and still others
Jeremiah or one of the prophets." He said to them,
"But who do you say that I am?" Simon Peter
answered, "You are the Messiah, the Son of the
living God."

—Matthew 16:13-16

This critical question Jesus asked his disciples comes to
us also: "Who do you say that I am?" The following exercise may help you begin to form an answer to that
question.

First, make a time line of your life, dividing your life
into three, four, or five sections—whatever makes the
most sense to you. To do this simply draw a line across
the page the long way and mark off sections by dates or
ages that define different periods in your life. If you are
keeping a journal, do this in your journal.

In each section record your impression of God during
that period, anything you remember learning about

God during those years, people who had a special influence on your beliefs, your understanding of prayer, etc. Record any spiritual experiences, either positive or negative, and any significant events that have taken place.

When you have finished, review what you have written, reflect on the following questions, and write what comes:

What changes do you see in your view of God? Be specific.

Did you encounter any unresolved issues as you reviewed your life? If so, what were they?

What changes would you still like to make in your spiritual life? Be specific.

If Jesus asked you now the same question he asked the disciples then, what would you say? "But who do you say that I am?"

Prayer Suggestion:

Offer to God your response to the question,
"Who do you say that I am?" Ask for God's
presence and for growth in your understanding
of who Jesus is.

Friday after Ash Wednesday

> Do not remember the former things, or consider the things of old. I am about to do a new thing; now it springs forth, do you not perceive it? I will make a way in the wilderness and rivers in the desert.
>
> I, I am He who blots out your transgressions for my own sake, and I will not remember your sins.
>
> —Isaiah 43:18-19, 25

Review your time line from yesterday again. As you look back over the periods in your life, are there incidents or memories or sins from the past that still hold you back—old hurts, resentments, anger—things that still nag deep inside, which still need to be confessed? Take a few minutes to review the time periods in your life and make a list of anything that comes to mind.

Is there any one incident or memory that stands out more than others? Write down what you feel as you remember.

Now reread the scripture for today several times and then offer the memories on your list to God, one by one, asking for God's cleansing and healing. Be still in God's presence. Hear his words of forgiveness. Record whatever comes to you.

Prayer Suggestion:

Continue your prayer by praying Psalm 51:1-17. When you have done this, reread the passage from Isaiah as your assurance of pardon. Give thanks to God. Record any other thoughts that come.

Saturday after Ash Wednesday

Beloved … this one thing I do: forgetting what lies behind and straining forward to what lies ahead, I press on toward the goal for the prize of the heavenly call of God in Christ Jesus.

—Philippians 3:13-14

Any time we go on a trip, we must decide what to take with us and what to leave behind. All too often we carry much more than we need and are weighed down by the excess.

The same is true with a spiritual journey or this journey through Lent. Now is a good time to examine old habits that weigh us down and decide which we might leave behind. (Habits can be both things we do and things we do not do!) Be quiet for a moment and see which habits surface. Jot them down. (It might help to review your time line again.)

Paul says if we die with Christ we will surely rise with him. Ask God to show you which habit is getting in the way of your growth the most. Be still and listen.

Record what comes to your mind. Also record your feelings as you listen.

What changes would you have to make to let go of this part of you? How would your life be different?

Sometimes the hard part is really wanting to change. Ask God to give you the courage to be willing to change, to let go.

Now ask for God's grace, God's empowerment, to let go of that which has come to mind so that you might be free of what you are giving up—free to experience resurrection as a new creation on Easter morning.

Prayer Suggestion:

Look back over what you have done in these four days, record any additional insights, and give God thanks for this time together.

First Sunday of Lent

Lectionary readings from Year A:

> Genesis 2:7-9; 3:1-7
> Psalm 51
> Romans 5:12-19
> Matthew 4:1-11

Lectionary readings from Year B:

> Genesis 9:8-15
> Psalm 25
> 1 Peter 3:18-22
> Mark 1:12-15

Lectionary readings from Year C:

> Deuteronomy 26:4-10
> Psalm 91
> Romans 10:8-13
> Luke 4:1-13

Reflecting on your Lenten journey, read the passages for this year, asking for God's illumination of the scripture. (1994 uses Year B, 1995 will use Year C, 1996 will use Year A, and so on.) Record any insights or prayers that come to you as you meditate on the passages.

Monday,
First Week of Lent

There is therefore now no condemnation for those who are in Christ Jesus.... For I am convinced that neither death, nor life, nor angels, nor rulers, nor things present, nor things to come, nor powers, nor height, nor depth, nor anything else in all creation, will be able to separate us from the love of God in Christ Jesus our Lord.

—Romans 8:1, 38-39

Sometimes when we go on a trip, we must travel on a toll road. There are usually one or more gates where we must stop to take a ticket or pay a toll. Too often we view spiritual disciplines during Lent as paying our toll or trying to make ourselves more acceptable. We do it to make up for our sins or to earn extra spiritual points. But there is no need for a toll road on a spiritual journey. What God has already given us in Jesus Christ has taken care of that. If we have chosen to give up something for Lent or have decided to let go of an old habit during Lent, the "giving up" is not for the purpose of paying the toll. What God has given us in Jesus Christ cannot

TO WALK WITH JESUS

be improved upon. Absolutely nothing can separate us from God's love.

The purpose of the Lenten journey is to help free us to be more open to the love and acceptance of God which are already present and to help us respond to that love more fully through our compassion for others.

Think back over your life (or review your time line again) and recall those evidences of God's love for you. Note the people and events that come to mind. Who are the people who have nurtured you? Through whom have you experienced God's love? What specifically did that person do to make you feel loved? Make a list as people come to mind.

What are the events that have had special significance in helping you know you are loved?

What is there in God's creation that speaks to you of God's love?

After listing those things that immediately come to mind, be still in God's presence and ask God to bring to mind other expressions of love for you. Jot down anything else that surfaces.

Prayer Suggestion:

Give thanks by lifting up to God each person, each event, and each part of God's creation that you have listed. Reflect on what God has given to us in Jesus Christ and again give thanks.

Tuesday,
First Week of Lent

For in hope we were saved. Now hope that is seen is not hope. For who hopes for what is seen? But if we hope for what we do not see, we wait for it with patience.

Likewise the Spirit helps us in our weakness; for we do not know how to pray as we ought, but that very Spirit intercedes with sighs too deep for words. And God, who searches the heart, knows what is the mind of the Spirit, because the Spirit intercedes for the saints according to the will of God.

—Romans 8:24-27

Any time we go on a trip, we have certain expectations, certain hopes about what will happen. The same is true with the spiritual journey. Take a few moments to think about what your hopes are for this Lenten journey. Write down whatever comes.

What do you hope for most?

What are your hopes about your life for the next month?

the next year?

the next five years?

Paul says that if we hope for something we wait for it with patience. Most of us would like to be more patient, but we want patience immediately!

God tells us through the prophet Isaiah, "My thoughts are not your thoughts, nor are your ways my ways, says the LORD. For as the heavens are higher than the earth, so are my ways higher than your ways" (55:8-9). We may not always understand God's timing, but God's timing is always perfect. The one who loves us most can see the whole picture.

Our hope is not rooted in our own psychological strength. The hope Paul is talking about is a hope rooted in the historic Christ event, a profound affirmation that there is light on the other side of darkness, there is life after death!

Prayer Suggestion:

We have the Spirit already interceding for us as we continue our journey. Pour out the hopes of your life to God; tell God your dreams for the future. Listen. Ask God to fill you with the dreams God has for you. Be still in God's presence and record whatever comes.

Wednesday,
First Week of Lent

The LORD will guide you continually, and satisfy
your needs in parched places, and make your bones
strong; and you shall be like a watered garden, like a
spring of water, whose waters never fail.

—Isaiah 58:11

Any time we go on a trip or a journey, we come to
crossroads or forks in the road somewhere along the
way. So it is with the spiritual journey. Sometimes the
way is clearly marked and sometimes there is no marker
at all. God promises continuing guidance, but sometimes discernment is hard.

Take a few minutes to think back through your life—
your time line may again be helpful here—and make a
list of those events or decisions that were definite turn-
ing points for you. List as many as you can. The list
might include things as obvious as deciding to marry or
not marry or things not so obvious, like being assigned
to a particular teacher in the third grade. Maybe something as simple as deciding to be more intentional in
your observation of Lent will be on your list.

When you have finished, review the list. What was your sense of God's presence in these events or decisions?

What options have been open to you because of the decision or event?

What options have been closed?

Are there doors once closed that call to you again? Are there talents long neglected that call you back to them?

Is God calling you to use your talents or gifts or abilities in a new way that might bring new life to you or to others? Be as specific as you can as you record what comes to you.

Prayer Suggestion:

God has promised to guide us continually. God has promised that we will be like a watered garden—growing, not dried up. Ask for God's guidance in claiming the gifts God has given you. Sit silently in God's presence. Record whatever comes.

Where or not to return to the Catholic Church
Getting Married
Having Children
Getting Married in the Church
Getting more involved in the Church
Home Schooling the Kids.

Thursday,
st Week of Lent

had come down from the mountain,
followed him; and there was a leper
him and knelt before him, saying,
choose, you can make me clean." He
it his hand and touched him, saying, "I
Be made clean!" Immediately his leprosy
d.

—Matthew 8:1-3

Jesus had just completed the sermon on the mount. He began that sermon with a list of encouragements for the downtrodden—blessed or happy are the poor in spirit, those who mourn, the meek, those who hunger and thirst ... for they shall be comforted, obtain mercy, be satisfied, be called children of God (see Matthew 5:1-10).

Jesus then tells the people—this gathering of good law-abiding followers—that he has come to fulfill the law not to abolish it. He spent most of the rest of the sermon telling them what he meant by these words. He spent most of the rest of his life showing them (and us) what he meant, and he began immediately. The first thing he did when he came down the mountain was break one of the oldest laws on the book. He touched a leper.

A leper was considered unclean, contaminating anything or anyone the leper touched. A leper was an outcast of the worst kind—feared, abhorred, shunned, banished from all human society—especially the temple.

Part of the miracle of the story is that the leper came to Jesus at all. The leper took the risk of approaching Jesus and the truth of who Jesus was began to unfold—Jesus' own journey to Jerusalem had begun.

In God's eyes, there are no untouchables. Who are the lepers of society today? Who are the outcasts, the feared, the ignored? Who is a leper for you? Reflect for a moment and jot down your response.

Is there someone you would rather ignore who is waiting for your attention, your acceptance, your presence? If someone comes to mind, jot down the name.

Could part of this Lenten journey be to go to that person and be or do whatever is needed?

What about the leper within? Are there old nodules of resentment, anger, mistrust, or guilt festering deep within which can cause alienation and isolation? Write down whatever surfaces.

Prayer Suggestion:

Offer what you have written to Jesus now. Replay the scripture story in your mind's eye. Then say to Jesus, "Lord, if you choose, you can make me whole." See his outstretched hand. Hear Jesus' words for you, "I will. Be clean." Record whatever comes.

Friday,
First Week of Lent

Now he was teaching in one of the synagogues on the sabbath. And just then there appeared a woman with a spirit that had crippled her for eighteen years. She was bent over and was quite unable to stand up straight. When Jesus saw her, he called her over and said, "Woman, you are set free from your ailment." When he laid his hands on her, immediately she stood up straight and began praising God.

—Luke 13:10-13

Christ set us free, so that we should remain free. Stand firm, then, and do not let yourselves be fastened again to the yoke of slavery.

—Galatians 5:1, *NJB*

There was an uproar from a ruler of the synagogue because Jesus healed this woman on the sabbath. Jesus' reply to him and the rest was, "You hypocrites! Does not each of you on the sabbath untie his ox or his donkey from the manger, and lead it away to give it water? And ought not this woman, a daughter of Abraham whom Satan bound for eighteen long years, be set free from this bondage on the sabbath day?" (Luke 13:15-16).

Again Jesus demonstrates what he means by fulfilling the law. He fulfills the law of love—love that sets us free.

The woman had been bent over for eighteen years. Jesus touched her and she was healed—set free, enabled to stand erect. Jesus calls to us in love. He wants us to be free of our infirmities. What are your infirmities, your bondage? Is it bondage to work? or other people's expectations? or food? or fear of failure? or pain? or caution? or ambition? or romance? or the clock? or some "should" or "ought"? or the fear of taking a risk? What is it that has you bent over? From what do you need to be freed? Be still with these questions and then write down whatever comes to mind in answer.

In your mind's eye, can you see yourself weighed down, bent over because of your bondage or addiction to whatever you have named? You might try drawing a figure bent over, loaded down by a bag of garbage. Then name the items in the bag. Be still. See Jesus coming toward you with his hand outstretched. What does he say to you? What do you say to him? Record whatever comes.

Prayer Suggestion:

Offer the load you are carrying to Jesus. Ask him to help you see yourself standing erect with the burden lifted. Stand or sit as erect as you can and give thanks.

Saturday,
First Week of Lent

I will look with favor upon you and make you fruitful and multiply you; and I will maintain my covenant with you. You shall eat old grain long stored, and you shall have to clear out the old to make way for the new. I will place my dwelling in your midst.... And I will walk among you, and will be your God, and you shall be my people. I am the LORD your God who brought you out of the land of Egypt, to be their slaves no more; I have broken the bars of your yoke and made you walk erect.

—Leviticus 26:9-13

So if anyone is in Christ, there is a new creation: everything old has passed away; see, everything has become new!

—2 Corinthians 5:17

"... Look, I am making the whole of creation new...."

—Revelations 21:5, *NJB*

The Bible is filled with God's promises to us to make us new creations. Review what you have written in this last week. How have you been eating the "old grain long stored"? What are those parts of your life that have brought and are bringing nourishment?

How have you been clearing "out the old to make way for the new"? Write down what you have done to make room for new opportunities or new ways of responding to life, new ways of growing into a "new creation."

What part of the old do you still need to clear out? Make a list. Does one thing on the list stand out more than the others?

Can you be specific about some areas of your life you would have God make new?

Prayer Suggestion:

Offer to God anything that you want God to transform. Ask for guidance if there is more that has surfaced that needs to be left behind. Give thanks for what has already been done. Sit in God's presence in silence. Write down whatever comes.

Review what you have done this week and record any additional insights that come.

Second Sunday of Lent

Lectionary readings from Year A:

> Genesis 12:1-4a
> Psalm 33
> 2 Timothy 1:8b-10
> Matthew 17:1-9

Lectionary readings from Year B:

> Genesis 22:1-2, 9a, 10-13, 15-18
> Psalm 116
> Romans 8:31b-34
> Mark 9:2-9

Lectionary readings from Year C:

> Genesis 15:5-12, 17-18
> Psalm 27
> Philippians 3:17—4:1
> Luke 9:28b-36

Reflecting on your Lenten journey, read the passages for this year, asking for God's illumination of the scripture. Record any insights or prayers that come to you as you meditate on the passages.

Monday, Second Week of Lent

"I am the good shepherd...."

—John 10:11

The LORD is my shepherd, I shall not want. He makes me lie down in green pastures; he leads me beside still waters; he restores my soul. He leads me in right paths for his name's sake.

Even though I walk through the darkest valley, I fear no evil; for you are with me; your rod and your staff—they comfort me.

You prepare a table before me in the presence of my enemies; you anoint my head with oil; my cup overflows. Surely goodness and mercy shall follow me all the days of my life, and I shall dwell in the house of the LORD my whole life long.

—Psalm 23

Throughout the Bible there are invitations to rest by still waters. Jesus models going apart to a quiet place. In the beginning of this Lenten focus was the invitation of Jesus to his disciples and to us to "come apart and rest a while."

TO WALK WITH JESUS

Reread the psalm slowly and prayerfully, remembering that Jesus is our shepherd. Try to imagine what it would be like to be led to good things, to be protected from danger. What image might you choose to express the kind of care and protection God provides if you were writing the psalm? Take a few minutes and try to write the psalm again as you would say it.

Jesus echoes the words of the psalmist in many different ways. The psalmist says, "Even though I walk through the darkest valley, I fear no evil; for you are with me" (v. 4). Many times Jesus says to his disciples and to us, "Fear not." Jesus' words are often more like a command than a suggestion. "Fear not! Do not be afraid for I am here beside you."

What have been some of your valleys? Be still and then list any valleys that surface.

What are the fears of your life? What is your greatest fear?

Is there a dark valley you face now?

Tell Jesus about the valley you face. Ask Jesus to walk through the valley with you, to meet you in this quiet place and give you peace instead of fear. Record whatever comes.

Give thanks for this quiet place. Rest by the still waters. Pray the psalm again.

Tuesday,
Second Week of Lent

I lift up my eyes to the hills—from where will my help come? My help comes from the LORD, who made heaven and earth. He will not let your foot be moved; he who keeps you will not slumber.

—Psalm 121:1-3

... [Jesus] went on ahead, going up to Jerusalem.

—Luke 19:28

A popular gospel song contains the refrain, "I'm coming up on the rough side of the mountain...." It is not unusual in our spiritual journey to come upon a mountain that must be climbed, walked around, or tunneled through. Whatever the obstacle before us, it often looks like the rough side of the mountain. The scenery may be beautiful from the top, but it is often difficult to get there.

Jesus was acquainted with mountains. The gospels tell us of Jesus' climb to Jerusalem, his climb to the Mount of Olives, and his climb up Golgotha's hill. None of these were easy climbs. Jesus knew where he was going and what must be done. Jesus never turned back even when the journey led to a cross.

What have been the mountains, the blocks, in your life? How have you experienced the presence of God as you look back at your mountains? What did you learn from the climb? Make a list as you remember.

What are the mountains before you now? What makes the mountain seem like the "rough side"? What help do you need if you are to climb? Be as specific as you can be.

Jesus promises to be with us always. He has climbed mountains before us and can already see the other side. Visualize if you can the mountain before you—however small or large it may be. Be still for a while. In your mind's eye, see Jesus going with you to the mountain. What do you do? What does Jesus do? What difference does Jesus' presence make? Record whatever comes.

Prayer Suggestion:

Be still and listen. Ask God to be with you as you face whatever mountain is before you. Prayerfully reread the words of the psalmist, pray the psalm, and hear God's promise to you again.

Wednesday, Second Week of Lent

Six days later, Jesus took with him Peter and James and his brother John and led them up a high mountain, by themselves. And he was transfigured before them, and his face shone like the sun, and his clothes became dazzling white. Suddenly there appeared to them Moses and Elijah, talking with him. Then Peter said to Jesus, "Lord, it is good for us to be here; if you wish, I will make three dwellings here, one for you, one for Moses, and one for Elijah." While he was still speaking, suddenly a bright cloud overshadowed them, and from the cloud a voice said, "This is my Son, the Beloved; with him I am well pleased; listen to him!" When the disciples heard this, they fell to the ground and were overcome by fear. But Jesus came and touched them, saying, "Get up and do not be afraid." And when they looked up, they saw no one except Jesus himself alone.

—Matthew 17:1-8

It is not unusual for God to speak on the mountaintop. Most of us have had an experience we might call a mountaintop experience—those times, often difficult to explain, when meaning or truth breaks through in some quiet or unexpected way and life is somehow changed. The experience may fade or lose intensity but the moment of truth cannot be denied.

What have been your mountaintops? Note them.

What happened after your mountaintop? What did you learn? How has that learning impacted your present life? Be as specific as you can be.

In the Biblical witness, the extraordinary is set in the middle of the ordinary. The mountaintops are surrounded by valleys—those places where we live and work and struggle to hear God's voice as everyday disciples. The same events precede the transfiguration story in Matthew, Mark, and Luke. Jesus had asked the disciples, "Who do you say that I am?" and the answer had been given—"You are the Christ." Then Jesus told them that he must go to Jerusalem and suffer and die. Just as the disciples thought they had it all together, everything fell apart again. In the midst of their confusion, Jesus invited them to the mountaintop.

Elijah and Moses appeared. The whole scene was so glorious that Peter made plans to stay. Even while Peter was making plans, a voice interrupts: "This is my Son, the Beloved; with him I am well pleased; listen to him!" Listen to him. Quit talking and listen.

In Matthew's gospel we are told that the disciples fell on their faces. Jesus touched them and told them, "Get up and do not be afraid"—not because there was nothing to fear but because he was with them. "Get up and try one more time," Jesus is saying. "Go back down the mountain with me and do not be afraid to be disciples."

Can you imagine yourself on that mountain with Jesus? Read the story again. What do you think you would have feared most if you had been on that mountain with Jesus? What do you fear now?

Prayer Suggestion:

Whether you are on the mountaintop or in the valley, tell Jesus where you are now. Tell him any confusion you may have about this journey or about who he is or how he relates to you. Tell him your fears. Hear his words to you, "Get up and do not be afraid." Hear God's words again, "Listen to him." "Listen to him." Write whatever comes.

Thursday, Second Week of Lent

Then [Jesus] said to them all, "If any want to become my followers, let them deny themselves and take up their cross daily and follow me. For those who want to save their life will lose it, and those who lose their life for my sake will save it. What does it profit them if they gain the whole world, but lose or forfeit themselves?"

—Luke 9:23-25

Immediately before this passage, Peter made his proclamation of faith, calling Jesus the Messiah, the Christ. Then Jesus told Peter and the other disciples that he must die. Jesus' next words are the words you have just read. If they would be followers of him, then they, too, must take up their crosses daily and follow. This is not an easy charge. For most of the rest of Luke's gospel, Jesus shows the disciples what he means. He heals the sick, he casts out demons, he eats with sinners, he lives love. Then he sends the disciples out to do the same.

Can you imagine what it would have been like to hear Jesus say these words to you? Reread the words from Luke and try to hear Jesus speaking them to you now. What do you feel as you hear Jesus speak the words, "take up [your] cross daily and follow me"? What is your cross? What does he say to you?

Glance through the rest of the gospel of Luke and make notes on what Jesus did.

Jesus sends the disciples out to live love. In what ways is Jesus calling you to live love? Be specific.

Who are you being called to love?

What changes can you make in your life to live love better?

What can you do this week?

Today?

Prayer Suggestion:

Each person's journey is different; each person's taking up the cross is different. Become quiet, asking God to bring to your mind the ways God would have you live love. Record whatever comes. Ask God for the courage and the grace to begin living love today, wherever God calls.

Friday,
Second Week of Lent

He was praying in a certain place, and after he had
finished, one of his disciples said to him, "Lord,
teach us to pray, as John taught his disciples." He
said to them, "When you pray, say:

Father, hallowed by your name.
> Your kingdom come.
> Give us each day our daily bread.
> And forgive us our sins,
> for we ourselves forgive everyone indebted to us.
> And do not bring us to the time of trial."

—Luke 11:1-4

"Pray then in this way:
Our Father in heaven,
> hallowed be your name.
> Your kingdom come.
> Your will be done,
> on earth as it is in heaven.
> Give us this day our daily bread.
> And forgive us our debts,
> as we also have forgiven our debtors.
> And do not bring us to the time of trial,
> but rescue us from the evil one."

—Matthew 6:9-13

"Lord, teach us to pray." Who among us on a spiritual journey has not longed to know more about prayer and how to pray? Look back at your time line for a moment. When in your life did you feel the closest to God? What was going on in your life at the time? What kinds of decisions or choices were you making? What place did prayer have in your life? Write any observations that come.

Are there any clues from the above prayer or examination of your time line that might inform your present spiritual journey? What is your prayer life like now? What do you long for most in understanding prayer or in being able to pray? Write what you long for as a request to Jesus.

Jesus was the master teacher. He modeled the importance of prayer as he daily sought time with God. Here Jesus gives us the model prayer. Read both versions of Jesus' prayer again. What are the parts of prayer that are included (e.g., petition, adoration, repentance, thanksgiving)? Make a note of these. How often do you include each part in your prayer life? Write a prayer now modeled after Jesus' prayer, or try rewriting the prayer in your own words.

Prayer Suggestion:

Ask Jesus to teach you to pray. Pray the prayers you have written, ending by slowly, thoughtfully praying the prayer Jesus taught us. Record any additional insights that come.

Saturday,
Second Week of Lent

"So I say to you, Ask, and it will be given you;
search, and you will find; knock, and the door will
be opened for you. For everyone who asks receives,
and everyone who searches finds, and for everyone
who knocks, the door will be opened. Is there
anyone among you who, if your child asks for a fish,
will give a snake instead of a fish? Or if the child
asks for an egg, will give a scorpion? If you then,
who are evil, know how to give good gifts to your
children, how much more will the heavenly Father
give the Holy Spirit to those who ask him!"

—Luke 11:9-13

Read also Luke 11:5-8 and Matthew 7:7-10.

Jesus continues teaching the disciples about prayer. He
has just taught the disciples the model prayer. Now he
tries to help them understand what talking to a loving
God is all about.

The verbs in this passage—ask, search, knock—have
the sense of persistence. Ask and keep on asking; search
and keep on searching; knock and keep on knocking.

Jesus has already shown us that there is more to prayer than just asking or searching or knocking, but he makes it clear in this passage that it is okay to ask.

What have you asked God for recently? How have you searched or knocked? What would you ask God for now?

What are those unanswered questions in your life for which you would like answers? What could searching for those answers mean to you now? On what doors do you still need to knock?

If you have started keeping a journal during this Lenten journey, it will be easier to keep up with your requests to God and the searching you may be doing. As answers or new insights come, go back and make a note by the prayer and date it.

Prayer Suggestion:

Ask God for the grace to know what to ask for, where to search, and when to knock.

Read back over what you have written. Come before God with each request, being still before God, listening for insight, waiting for grace.

Review what you have done this week and record any additional insights that come during this time of prayer.

Third Sunday of Lent

Lectionary readings from Year A:

    Exodus 17:3-7
    Psalm 95
    Romans 5:1-2, 5-8
    John 4:5-42

Lectionary readings from Year B:

    Exodus 20:1-17
    Psalm 19
    1 Corinthians 1:22-25
    John 2:13-25

Lectionary readings from Year C:

    Exodus 3:1-8a, 13-15
    Psalm 103
    1 Corinthians 10:1-6, 10-12
    Luke 13:1-9

Reflecting on your Lenten journey, read the passages for this year, asking for God's illumination of the scripture. Record any insights or prayers that come to you as you meditate on the passages.

Monday,
Third Week of Lent

The day was drawing to a close, and the twelve came to him and said, "Send the crowd away, so that they may go into the surrounding villages and countryside, to lodge and get provisions; for we are here in a deserted place." But he said to them, "You give them something to eat." They said, "We have no more than five loaves and two fish—unless we are to go and buy food for all these people." For there were about five thousand men. And he said to his disciples, "Make them sit down in groups of about fifty each." They did so and made them all sit down. And taking the five loaves and the two fish, he looked up to heaven, and blessed and broke them, and gave them to the disciples to set before the crowd. And all ate and were filled. What was left over was gathered up, twelve baskets of broken pieces.

—Luke 9:12-17

You may also want to read Matthew 14:13-21, Mark 6:30-44, or John 6:1-13.

This is the only miracle of Jesus recorded in all four gospels. There must be something important the gospel writers wanted us to hear!

Just before this story begins, the disciples had just completed a long and tiring journey; they had been teaching and healing and casting out demons and preaching in Jesus' name. The scriptures tells us that they had not even had time to eat. On top of that, they had just learned of the beheading of their friend, John the Baptist, and they had stopped by to bury him on the way home.

When Jesus saw the weary group, he understood their fatigue and invited them to come away with him to rest a while. But the crowds figured out where they were going and got to the other side of the lake before them. Jesus cared about his disciples, but Jesus also had compassion for the crowds so he stopped to minister to them. Jesus taught them and healed them.

The hour grew late and the tired, hungry disciples urged Jesus to send the crowd away because it was supper time and there was no food. Jesus told them to feed the crowd. "Feed them? How?" the disciples questioned. "Find what you can," Jesus answered.

The gospel writers tell us that a little boy had five loaves and two fish—not much to feed all those people. But he gave the disciples what he had—and you know the rest of the story. Jesus blessed the loaves and the fish and broke them and gave them to the disciples to feed the hungry crowd. And there were twelve baskets of food left over—enough to feed those twelve hungry disciples.

Of all the things that one could say about this story, two things are very clear. First, Jesus intended that all the people be fed, and he expected his disciples to participate in the feeding. Second, Jesus was able to take what appeared to be a very small gift from a small boy and work a miracle.

Who are the people pressing around you that Jesus may be asking you to help feed? The need may be for physical food, but the greater need might be for a word of kindness, encouragement, a visit, a note, etc. Be still and let God bring to mind those needs which are most pressing. Write down whatever comes.

What are the special gifts God has given you? Make a list. If you have trouble making a list, ask God to bring to mind those special gifts God has given to you—however small they may seem to you. Write down anything that surfaces.

To Walk With Jesus

Prayer Suggestion:

Review the list you have just made. Now one by one offer the gifts God has given you to Jesus, asking him to bless and multiply each one. Offer to him the needs that have surfaced and ask him now how he wants you to use your gifts to meet those needs. Listen. Then ask for grace and courage to begin where he leads. Write down any additional insights that may come during this time of listening.

Tuesday,
Third Week of Lent

When evening came, his disciples went down to the sea, got into a boat, and started across the sea to Capernaum. It was now dark, and Jesus had not yet come to them. The sea became rough because a strong wind was blowing. When they had rowed about three or four miles, they saw Jesus walking on the sea and coming near the boat, and they were terrified. But he said to them, "It is I; do not be afraid."

—John 6:16-20

Read also Mark 6:45-52 or Matthew 14:22-27.

The five thousand had just been fed. Jesus then sent the disciples to the other side of the lake while he went up the mountain to pray. As evening came, the disciples were out on the sea, rowing against an adverse wind. Jesus saw them and the scriptures tell us that he walked on water toward them. They were all frightened, thinking they were seeing a ghost. Jesus said to them, "Take heart, it is I; do not be afraid" (Mark 6:50). He stepped in the boat and the sea was calm again.

How often do we find ourselves on our own stormy seas, rowing hard against adverse winds? As hard as we row, or as hard as we may try, we do not seem to get anywhere. Have there been times when you were trying so hard that when help came you did not even recognize it?

Is there any challenge in your life now that you have tried to change, or maybe you want to change and don't know how to try? Is there any area of your life in which the strong, adverse winds blow hard inside, making it difficult to feel calm, to feel at peace? Be still with these questions and record whatever comes.

Visualize Jesus coming to you on your own turbulent sea. As you feel yourself tossed to and fro, tell him about the winds, the rough seas in your life. What do you say to him? What does he say to you? Can you hear his words to you, "Take heart, it is I; do not be afraid"?

Prayer Suggestion:

Be quiet for a while. Be open to hearing Jesus' words for you. Remember that Jesus stepped in the boat with his disciples. He always makes himself available to us where we are. See him step into your boat. Feel his calm as the hard winds cease. Give him thanks for his presence. Record whatever comes.

Wednesday, Third Week of Lent

They came to Bethsaida. Some people brought a blind man to him and begged him to touch him. He took the blind man by the hand and led him out of the village; and when he had put saliva on his eyes and laid his hands on him, he asked him, "Can you see anything?" And the man looked up and said, "I can see people, but they look like trees, walking." Then Jesus laid his hands on his eyes again; and he looked intently and his sight was restored, and he saw everything clearly.

—Mark 8:22-25

See also John 9:1-7.

Most of us who are serious about our Lenten journey have had Jesus touch our lives in some way. It may have been dramatic and immediately life-changing. Or it may have been very gradual—the kind of change that happens slowly, step by tiny step until our lives are completely different. Most of us have experienced moments of spiritual blindness when the way ahead was unclear or could not be seen at all. Again insight may have come suddenly, clearing the way ahead, or it may have come

TO WALK WITH JESUS

step by tiny step. The slower change or "seeing" is depicted in this story.

The blind man was brought to Jesus, who touched him and asked him if he could see. He replied that he could see, but not very clearly—people looked like trees. Jesus touched him again and "he looked intently and his sight was restored, and he saw everything clearly."

Review your time line again. Are there times when your faith seemed crystal clear?

Were there times when faith existed, but was cloudy or unclear?

Were there times when you could not see at all?

What is your current faith experience? Are there areas of faith that once seemed clear but have now become cloudy? Are there areas that once were cloudy but now seem more clear? Are there areas in your faith experience in which you cannot see at all? Where do you most need Jesus' second touch? Be still with these questions and write down whatever comes. Be as specific as you can.

Now ask for Jesus' healing or for Jesus' second touch wherever there is need. Be still in his presence and give thanks.

Thursday,
Third Week of Lent

Now in Jerusalem by the Sheep Gate there is a pool, called in Hebrew Beth-zatha, which has five porticoes. In these lay many individuals—blind, lame, and paralyzed. One man was there who had been ill for thirty-eight years. When Jesus saw him lying there and knew that he had been there a long time, he said to him, "Do you want to be made well?" The sick man answered him, "Sir, I have no one to put me into the pool when the water is stirred up; and while I am making my way, someone else steps down ahead of me." Jesus said to him, "Stand up, take your mat and walk." At once the man was made well, and he took up his mat and began to walk.

—John 5:2-9

The place was a pool called Beth-zatha. The blind, the lame, and the paralyzed waited by the pool for the waters to be moved. One ancient source tells us that at certain seasons an angel of the Lord went down into the pool and troubled the water; whoever stepped in first, after the troubling of the water, was healed of whatever had been wrong.

This man had been by the pool for thirty-eight years. Jesus knew that he had been there for a long time, so he asked the man the question, "Do you want to be made well?" The man did not simply reply "yes." He walked around Jesus' question by answering that he had no one to help him and someone always got down the steps before him. Few would doubt this man really wanted to be healed. But his answer to Jesus' question leaves us wondering why he did not answer directly.

The man had been by the pool for thirty-eight years. We could guess that this was probably most of his life. To be healed now would mean learning a whole new way of behavior—a new way of life.

Sometimes it's scary to let go of old patterns, old habits, old addictions. We want change. We want to be healed, but we are afraid sometimes to take the steps necessary to help change occur. Are there habits which have long been with you that you find hard to change or let go?

Are there old relationships that have long been negative and badly need healing? Are you afraid to try again? Do you want to be healed? Be still with the questions for a few minutes and make a note of whatever comes.

Jesus saw the man's predicament. Even when the man gave Jesus his excuses, Jesus knew what he

　　　　　　　　　　　　　TO WALK WITH JESUS

needed. When Jesus was present, there was no need for others to get him to the pool when the water was stirred. Jesus had compassion on him and said, "Stand up, take your mat and walk." The man immediately did as he was told; he was healed. In what area of your life would you most like to hear Jesus say to you, "Stand up to whatever is holding you back, take your mat or whatever is necessary, and walk.... Be healed of whatever is holding you back; get on with your life"?

Prayer Suggestion:

Be quiet for a moment, open to God's leading. Hear Jesus' question for you—"Do you want to be made well?" What is your answer? What are you willing to do? What are you willing to let Jesus do for you? Engage Jesus in dialogue. Record whatever comes.

Friday,
Third Week of Lent

[Jesus] entered Jericho and was passing through it. A man was there named Zacchaeus; he was a chief tax collector and was rich. He was trying to see who Jesus was, but on account of the crowd he could not, because he was short in stature. So he ran ahead and climbed a sycamore tree to see him, because he was going to pass that way. When Jesus came to the place, he looked up and said to him, "Zacchaeus, hurry and come down; for I must stay at your house today." So he hurried down and was happy to welcome him. All who saw it began to grumble and said, "He has gone to be the guest of one who is a sinner." Zacchaeus stood there and said to the Lord, "Look, half of my possessions, Lord, I will give to the poor; and if I have defrauded anyone of anything, I will pay back four times as much." Then Jesus said to him, "Today salvation has come to this house, because he too is a son of Abraham. For the Son of Man came to seek out and to save the lost."

—Luke 19:1-10

Zacchaeus had to make extra effort to see Jesus. He was a short man and could not see over the crowds. Zacchaeus also was disliked by the people because he was a rich tax collector—a chief sinner in the eyes of the people. Zacchaeus climbed the tree in order to see Jesus—a climb well worth making because Jesus saw him, beckoned him to come down from the tree and be his host. The crowds did not like Jesus going to the home of such a sinner.

For Zacchaeus the encounter with Jesus was a transforming experience. Jesus had called him by name. To be with Jesus was to change his way of living. Zacchaeus pledged to give one-half of all he had to the poor and to give back four times what he had taken to anyone he had cheated. Jesus showed Zacchaeus and all the people that he came to save the lost.

It is not unusual in scripture to see Jesus encountering and interacting with the marginal people of society. Over and over again he fulfills Isaiah's prophecy that he would bind up the broken hearted, bring release to the captives, and make the blind see.

Have you ever felt like one of the marginal people of society? Have you ever felt like an outcast, like you had to try harder, climb higher, just to see what others saw? If you have such a memory or even now feel like an outcast in some area of your life, in your mind's eye, climb into the nearest tree and see Jesus coming. Hear him call your name. Come down to him and listen to him. Know how much he loves you. Record whatever comes.

Who are those you consider the outcast or the marginal people of society? Who are the people you would rather avoid? Is there any person or group of people who might need your help to climb a little higher to see Jesus more clearly? How might you make a difference in the life of another? Make a note of whatever comes.

Prayer Suggestion:

Be still in God's presence. Tell Jesus those ways you feel unloved or unlovely and ask for his transforming visit. If you find yourself as one of the angry crowd, ask for Jesus' help in loving as he loved. Ask Jesus to help you see more clearly who God would love through you. Ask for courage and grace to act on what he shows you.

Saturday,
Third Week of Lent

On the way to Jerusalem Jesus was going through
the region between Samaria and Galilee. As he
entered a village, ten lepers approached him. Keeping their distance, they called out, saying, "Jesus,
Master, have mercy on us!" When he saw them, he
said to them, "Go and show yourselves to the
priests." And as they went, they were made clean.
Then one of them, when he saw that he was healed,
turned back, praising God with a loud voice. He
prostrated himself at Jesus' feet and thanked him.

—Luke 17:11-16

Jesus is still on the way to Jerusalem. The lepers come
and ask for healing. Jesus sends them on their way to
have the priests examine them. (Lepers were considered
unclean in every area of life. A leper was ritually unclean and could not enter the temple unless the priest
pronounced the leper clean.) This story is one incident
in Jesus' healing ministry when the person or persons
are not healed instantly. The story tells us that as they
followed Jesus' instructions, the healing came. "As they
went," Luke tells us, "they were made clean."

During this Lenten journey, you have been asked to focus several times on those parts of your life that need healing, those places which fester within that still need God's healing touch. Review what you have written. Have there been times in this Lenten journey when you have felt God's special presence, God's healing touch?

Look back at your time line for a moment. Have there been times as you look back on your life where healing or growth or change has come when you simply kept plugging away, doing whatever you needed to do?

Are there places now in your life where there is a call to obedience? Is God calling you to a special task that may be the vehicle used for your healing or growth? Are there things that need doing which for too long have been left undone? Are you ready to participate in your own healing? Make a note of whatever comes.

Only one of the healed lepers paused to say thanks. For what do you still need to thank God? Are there other people you still need to thank? Make a note of any names that come to mind and make a plan for giving thanks.

TO WALK WITH JESUS

Prayer Suggestion:

Review your Lenten journey thus far and think about your present life. Spend time giving God thanks for those special moments of the Spirit's presence in this journey. Be specific.

Fourth Sunday of Lent

Lectionary readings from Year A:

    1 Samuel 16:1b, 6-7, 10-13a
    Psalm 23
    Ephesians 5:8-14
    John 9:1-41

Lectionary readings from Year B:

    2 Chronicles 36:14-16, 19-23
    Psalm 137
    Ephesians 2:4-10
    John 3:14-21

Lectionary readings from Year C:

    Joshua 5:9a, 10-12
    Psalm 34
    2 Corinthians 5:17-21
    Luke 15:1-3, 11-32

Reflecting on your Lenten journey, read the passages for this year, asking for God's illumination of the scripture. Record any insights or prayers that come to you as you meditate on the passages.

Monday,
Fourth Week of Lent

Now there was a woman who had been suffering
from hemorrhages for twelve years; and though she
had spent all she had on physicians, no one could
cure her. She came up behind [Jesus] and touched
the fringe of his clothes, and immediately her hemor-
rhage stopped.... Jesus said, "Someone touched me;
for I noticed that power had gone out from me."
When the woman saw that she could not remain hidden, she came trembling; and falling down before
him, she declared in the presence of all the people
why she had touched him, and how she had been
immediately healed. He said to her, "Daughter, your
faith has made you well; go in peace."

—Luke 8:43-48

Jesus was on his way to heal Jairus' daughter. A great
crowd followed him. In that crowd was a woman who
had been suffering from hemorrhages for twelve years.
In the Jewish law, blood symbolized life (Leviticus
17:11), but when a woman was bleeding, she was considered unclean or impure for seven days or for as long
as the flow continued. Anyone or anything she touched

TO WALK WITH JESUS

was also considered unclean and must go through a ritual of purification (Leviticus 15:19-27).

For twelve years, this woman had known isolation—she had not been touched or hugged or held. She could not enter the temple or associate with others. She had tried doctors everywhere and had used up all of her financial resources. She was physically, emotionally, and financially drained. Can you imagine how she might have felt?

What are the things that drain you of life, that leave you exhausted? Is there something in your life that has drained you for a long time?

What are the things in your life that isolate you or make you feel isolated from others?

The woman in this story must have already heard stories about Jesus healing people. It was a great risk for her to go into the crowd and take the chance of being recognized. She might have been publicly shunned and humiliated. Not only was she unclean, it was also un-lawful for a woman to touch a man in public. But those were risks she was willing to take to be healed.

Just to be able to touch the hem of his garment—that would be enough she thought—enough to make her whole. And then she could slip away into the crowd undetected. But it didn't work that way. Jesus knew something had happened and called her forth. Trembling she admitted touching him and confessed her healing. Jesus acknowledged her risk of faith and said to her, "Daughter, your faith has made you well; go in peace."

In what area of your life do you most need to hear Jesus' words to you, "Your faith has made you well"? What needs to be done? What can you do? What risk is involved? Be still with the questions and write down whatever comes.

Prayer Suggestion:

Reread the story. Try to feel what the woman must have felt. Acknowledge Jesus' healing presence. Tell him any ways you feel drained or isolated. Ask him for wisdom and courage to take any risks you need to take to participate in your wholeness. Record any additional reflections.

Tuesday,
Fourth Week of Lent

When he had finished speaking he said to Simon,
"Put out into deep water and pay out your nets for a
catch." Simon replied, "Master, we worked hard all
night long and caught nothing, but if you say so, I
will pay out the nets." And when they had done
this, they netted such a huge number of fish that
their nets began to tear....

—Luke 5:4-7, *NJB*

The crowds were following Jesus, clamoring to get
nearer to hear him teach, to receive his healing. Jesus
spotted the weary fishermen, stooping in the quiet ritual
of cleaning their empty nets after a long night of fishing.
Jesus stepped in Peter's boat and asked him to push it
out a little from the shore so he could teach the people
from the boat. When Jesus finished teaching, he asked
Peter to go out again and cast the nets into the deep
waters.

"Fishing again?" You can almost hear Peter grumble,
"but Master, we have fished all night!" But even in his
reluctance, Peter is obedient. "But if you say so, I will
pay out the nets." And the nets overflowed with fish.

How many times do we resist trying again? It's hard to learn lessons slowly, painfully, to cover the same territory again and again. A friend recently told me the story of putting her sleepy-eyed four-year-old to bed and going downstairs, finally able to prop up her feet and read a good book. Before she could find the place in the book, she heard a loud thump followed by a loud wail. She dashed back up the stairs. By the time she appeared in the room, her son was sitting on the bed, grinning sheepishly. Only a tear left on the cheek betrayed where the wail had come from. His arms reached up to her and said, "It's okay, Mommy. I just stayed too close to where I got in. I'll crawl in deeper this time."

Maybe that is what God is calling us to do this Lenten season—just crawl in a little deeper, to bring the whole of who we are to him, not to come in just part of the way, but to cast our nets into the deep one more time.

Have there been times when, like the fishermen, you have found yourself wearily trying to clean the empty nets in your life, when you have tried as hard as you knew how and still there was nothing to show for the effort? Are there places God may be calling you to come deeper?

Is there something God may be calling you to try one more time? What kind of effort is necessary on your part? What will it mean for you to push out into the deep one more time? Be still and listen. Record whatever comes. Be as specific as you can.

> ## *Prayer Suggestion:*
>
> Bring to God whatever has surfaced. Be still in God's presence. Ask God for the grace to know how to come deeper, where to let the nets down one more time to be filled. Record any additional insights that come in the quiet.

Wednesday,
Fourth Week of Lent

> Martha said to Jesus, "Lord, if you had been here,
> my brother would not have died." ... Jesus said to
> her, "I am the resurrection and the life. Those who
> believe in me, even though they die, will live, and
> everyone who lives and believes in me will never
> die. Do you believe this?"
>
> —John 11:21, 25-26

Sometimes on a journey we come to a sign in the road
that says "caution ahead." So it was as Jesus received
word that Lazarus was ill. To go to Lazarus meant to
return to a place where the people had already tried to
stone him. But it was important for Jesus to go. Jesus
loved Mary and Martha and Lazarus. He cared about
their pain. He was willing to take the risk of returning.

By the time Jesus arrived, Lazarus was already dead.
Martha greeted Jesus with, "If you had been here, my
brother would not have died." Mary fell at his feet, "If
you had been here ...." Jesus responded to their "if
onlys" with "I am ...." "I am the resurrection and the
life." I am the resurrection and the life now. I am the

resurrection and the life on this side of the grave as well as beyond. "Do you believe this?"

Jesus' question to Martha is asked of us as well—Do *you* believe this? We go through our lives with so many "if onlys." If only I were smarter or prettier or more handsome or smaller or taller or stronger or had more money or lived in a different place or were more talented. If only my spouse or my friend or my boss or my child or my parent understood me better, or would change the way they … or would stop doing … or would try harder to … or would start doing ….

What are the "if onlys" of your life—those things you wish were different? Make a list of them.

Jesus came to Martha and Mary in the midst of death and promised life. He heard their "if onlys" and responded with "I am." I am resurrection. I am life. He comes to us too in the midst of our deserts, our dry places, our grief, our pain, our brokenness. He knows and hears each of our "if onlys."

Try to envision Jesus coming to you. Lift to him each thing on your list one by one. Say to him, "Jesus, if only …" and as you go down your list, listen. Hear what he would say to you. Record whatever comes.

Prayer Suggestion:

Be still in Jesus' presence. Hear his question to you, "Do you believe?" What is your answer? If it is hard to answer "yes," ask for his help, his grace, to believe as you journey toward resurrection and new life.

Thursday, Fourth Week of Lent

So they took the stone away.... [Jesus] cried in a loud
voice, "Lazarus, come out!" The dead man came out,
his feet and hands bound with strips of material,
and a cloth over his face. Jesus said to them, "Unbind him, let him go free."

—John 11:41a, 43-44, *NJB*

Jesus came to the tomb of Lazarus when he had already
been dead four days. In that climate, four days was long
enough for the body to begin to decay. Over Martha's
warning, Jesus asked the people to take the stone away.
He then called to Lazarus in a loud voice. Lazarus came
out, still bound by the grave clothes. Jesus said to the
people, "Unbind him, let him go free."

There are times in our spiritual journeys when an
event or the circumstances of our lives hold us entombed. We feel more dead than alive. At other times
we know we have heard Jesus call us to come forth in
new life. We see a glimmer of hope but we are still
bound by the grave clothes. Where are you now? Are
you still entombed, longing to hear Jesus call your name
and call you forth to new life? Are you standing outside

the tomb, but still bound in some way by the unknown, apathy, fear, distrust, self-doubt, a need to control others, self-centeredness, or unhealed memories? Be still with the questions, then write whatever comes to you.

If you are still in the tomb, ask Jesus to help you know what holds you entombed. Listen to Jesus call your name to come forth. If you have already heard Jesus call you forth but are standing on the outside of the tomb still bound, tell him how you are still bound, how you still need to be set free.

Jesus calls Lazarus forth to new life. He tells the people to unbind him, to unwrap the grave clothes. How might Jesus be calling you to help unbind another? How, as the body of Christ, can we participate in setting others free? Write down any thoughts or insights that come to you.

Prayer Suggestion:

Envision yourself bound in the grave clothes. Imagine whatever has surfaced today written on the grave clothes—i.e., self-doubt, worry, fear. Hear Jesus call your name again, calling you to new life. Feel the grave clothes begin to come off and fall at your feet. Rejoice. Give thanks for what God is doing in your life. Ask for greater awareness of how we as a church can participate in setting others free. Be still and listen. Record whatever comes.

Friday,
Fourth Week of Lent

Then he told this parable: "A man had a fig tree planted in his vineyard; and he came looking for fruit on it and found none. So he said to the gardener, 'See here! For three years I have come looking for fruit on this fig tree, and still I find none. Cut it down! Why should it be wasting the soil?' He replied, 'Sir, let it alone for one more year, until I dig around it and put manure on it. If it bears fruit next year, well and good; but if not, you can cut it down.'"

—Luke 13:6-9

By contrast, the fruit of the Spirit is love, joy, peace, patience, kindness, generosity, faithfulness, gentleness, and self-control.... If we live by the Spirit, let us also be guided by the Spirit.

—Galatians 5:22-23a, 25

When Jesus calls us to new life, he calls us to be new creations. Jesus tells the disciples many parables on the way to Jerusalem. He tries to show them and tell them what it looks like to be a new creation in him.

During this Lenten season, we have often focused on letting go of those parts of ourselves that hold us back

TO WALK WITH JESUS

and keep us from being all that we are called to be. But even as we let go of the old, Jesus makes it clear in this parable that there is something new we are to take on. How have you been "wasting the soil"? What needs pruning from your life that you may bear more fruit? What is the fruit Jesus would have you bear?

Focus for a while on the words of Paul as he lists for us the fruits of the Spirit. Which of the fruits do you already possess? Which need more fertilizer and cultivation? Which do you still need to receive? Write down whatever comes.

Prayer Suggestion:

Begin by becoming quiet and then giving thanks for all God has already given you. Ask God to bring to mind which fruit of the Spirit God would most like to cultivate in your life now. Ask for the grace to hear God's desire for you and for openness to growing as God would have you grow. Record any insights that come.

Saturday,
Fourth Week of Lent

"I am the true vine, and my Father is the vinegrower. He removes every branch in me that bears no fruit. Every branch that bears fruit he prunes to make it bear more fruit.... Abide in me as I abide in you. Just as the branch cannot bear fruit by itself unless it abides in the vine, neither can you unless you abide in me. I am the vine, you are the branches. Those who abide in me and I in them bear much fruit, because apart from me you can do nothing.... As the Father has loved me, so I have loved you; abide in my love. If you keep my commandments, you will abide in my love, just as I have kept my Father's commandments and abide in his love. I have said these things to you so that my joy may be in you, and that your joy may be complete. This is my commandment, that you love one another as I have loved you."

—John 15:1-2, 4-5, 9-12

Jesus makes it clear in this passage that we cannot bear fruit unless we abide in him—unless we receive our strength and energy from him. We cannot just decide to

TO WALK WITH JESUS

bear fruit and have fruit suddenly appear. Our part is to stay connected to Jesus, to sit in his presence and allow his love and his commandments to cultivate us for bearing fruit.

Read back over what you have written for the last week. What is Jesus healing? What areas of your life are being cultivated for new growth? What areas are being pruned or still need pruning? Where do you most need cultivation? Be still in God's presence and write whatever comes.

Jesus tells us to abide in his love and he tells us that keeping his commandments is one way to abide in his love. Jesus says that he is telling us about this so "that our joy may be complete." What does it mean to you for your joy to be complete? Is this a present reality? If not, reread the passage and see if you find any clues that could make a difference. Make notes of any insights that come as you reread the passage.

Prayer Suggestion:

Be still in God's presence. Feel God's love for you. Ask for a deeper understanding and the experience of "abiding in him." Open yourself for whatever God has for you. Open yourself for growth as God leads. Record whatever comes.

Review what you have done this week and record any additional insights that come.

Fifth Sunday of Lent

Lectionary readings from Year A:

> Ezekiel 37:12-14
> Psalm 130
> Romans 8:8-11
> John 11:1-45

Lectionary readings from Year B:

> Jeremiah 31:31-34
> Psalm 51
> Hebrews 5:7-9
> John 12:20-33

Lectionary readings from Year C:

> Isaiah 43:16-21
> Psalm 126
> Philippians 3:8-14
> John 8:1-11

Reflecting on your Lenten journey, read the passages for this year, asking for God's illumination of the scripture. Record any insights or prayers that come to you as you meditate on the passages.

Monday,
Fifth Week of Lent

Then one of the twelve, who was called Judas Iscariot, went to the chief priests and said, "What will
you give me if I betray him to you?" They paid him
thirty pieces of silver. And from that moment he
began to look for an opportunity to betray him....
When it was evening, [Jesus] took his place with the
twelve; and while they were eating, he said, "Truly I
tell you, one of you will betray me." And they became greatly distressed and began to say to him one
after another, "Surely not I, Lord?" He answered,
"The one who has dipped his hand into the bowl
with me will betray me." … Judas, who betrayed
him, said, "Surely not I, Rabbi?" He replied, "You
have said so."

—Matthew 26:14-16, 20-23, 25

"One of you will betray me," Jesus tells them, and the
questions begin. "Not I?" "Not I?" "Not I?" It is easy to
wonder how Judas could have asked that question. Was
he testing Jesus to see if Jesus could somehow know
what he had done? Could it have been a question of
utter disbelief—"Could I really do what I have done?
Can I really do what I am about to do?" And Judas

leaned over and dipped the bread with Jesus, "Surely not I, Rabbi?"

We know the rest of the story. After Jesus was condemned, Judas repented, and went back to return the thirty pieces of silver, declaring, "I have betrayed innocent blood." And he went out and hanged himself (Matthew 27:3-10).

Judas' question is a question for each one of us— "Surely not I?" How have we betrayed another? Is it possible that we, too, have betrayed Jesus? Stay with the question in silence for a moment asking Jesus, "Surely not I?" Record whatever comes.

Judas wanted to take back the words that would not come back. He wanted to correct the deed he could not correct. Judas repented, but Judas failed to recognize Jesus' forgiving love.

Have there ever been times when you have spoken words that you wished you could take back, but they would not come back? Have there been times when you have done something you deeply regretted, but had to live with the fact that the deed was done? Such memories can be painful, but the memory can also be healed.

Judas acted hastily and never got to hear Jesus' words from the cross, "Father, forgive them; for they do not know what they are doing." If a word or a deed surfaces for which you have not experienced God's forgiving love, stop and tell God what you remember and ask for forgiveness now. Imagine Jesus standing before you; hear him speak the words, "Father, forgive _____" and hear Jesus call your name. Ask God to help you hear Jesus' words, "Father, forgive them," as words spoken for you.

Prayer Suggestion:

Be in God's presence and feel God's love for you just as you are. Hear Jesus' words spoken to you—"Father, forgive." Receive God's forgiveness. Give thanks. Record whatever comes.

Tuesday,
Fifth Week of Lent

Then Jesus went with them to a place called Gethsemane; and he said to his disciples, "Sit here while I go over there and pray." He took with him Peter and the two sons of Zebedee, and began to be grieved and agitated. Then he said to them, "I am deeply grieved, even to death; remain here, and stay awake with me." And going a little farther, he threw himself on the ground and prayed, "My Father, if it is possible, let this cup pass from me; yet not what I want but what you want."

—Matthew 26:36-39

See also Mark 14:32-36 and Luke 22:40-42.

When Jesus and his disciples finished supper, they sang a hymn and then went together to the Mount of Olives, to a garden called Gethsemane. By this time the disciples must have been confused and exhausted, having just heard Jesus talk of his betrayal and death. Jesus asked them to stay awake with him and then he left them to wrestle with ultimate submission. The disciples were soon fast asleep.

Nothing penetrated the disciples' sleep, not even Jesus' anguished cry, "My Father, if it be possible, let this cup pass from me"—or as it might be translated, "Daddy, Daddy, I don't want to go through this if there is any other way." Jesus' cry was a cry that still echoes through the centuries into the dark night of every soul who struggles to change that which cannot be changed—"if it be possible, if it be possible!"

Have there been times in your own life when in the agony of the moment you have cried out to God, "If it be possible, if it be possible, change all that is going on, change what I must do, change what I have done"? What have been your moments of darkness, of difficult decision, of temptation? What were the circumstances? What do you feel as you remember? Make a note of what comes.

As the disciples slept, Jesus continued to pray, to struggle. Release came in that ultimate gut-wrenching surrender which separated heaven and hell, life and death, defeat and hope—not what I want, but what you want, Father. Then Jesus went back to wake the disciples to say good-bye.

The garden was a lonely place, even though friends were with Jesus, for ultimately the act of surrender was his alone. So it is with us. There are some things no one can do for us. Jesus has felt our pain before us. His surrender made the difference between death and life, defeat and hope. Is there a struggle in your life that needs to be released to him? What do you need to say to Jesus?

Prayer Suggestion:

Be with Jesus in the garden. Hear his cry. Offer to him any struggle of your life. Know his understanding and love for you. Record whatever comes.

Wednesday,
Fifth Week of Lent

While [Jesus] was still speaking, Judas, one of the
twelve, arrived; with him was a large crowd with
swords and clubs, from the chief priests and the
elders of the people. Now the betrayer had given
them a sign, saying, "The one I will kiss is the man;
arrest him." At once he came up to Jesus and said,
"Greetings, Rabbi!" and kissed him. Jesus said to
him, "Friend, do what you are here to do." Then
they came and laid hands on Jesus and arrested
him.... Then all the disciples deserted him and fled.

—Matthew 26:47-50, 56b

It all happened so fast. Just hours before they were
preparing and celebrating the Passover meal together.
Now their friend, the one they had trusted, had believed
to be the answer to their hope, had been arrested, led
away by guards. To make matters worse, one of their
own was the betrayer. What was there to do but flee?
Who could be trusted? What could be trusted? A journey that had led to apparent triumph a few days ago as
they entered Jerusalem now seemed to be leading to dis-
aster. Everything had fallen apart.

Have there been times in your own life when everything seemed to be falling apart, when all that you once counted on changed and it was difficult to know which way to turn next? Has there been a time when you felt like running away? What did you do? What do you feel as you remember? Make a note of whatever comes.

Jesus was betrayed by a kiss by one with whom he had shared his life and his ministry of love. Then all of his friends, the ones with whom he had shared his life intimately, ran away. Have there been times in your life when you have felt betrayed, forsaken? Make a note of whatever comes.

Can you imagine yourself in that garden at the time of the arrest? What would you have done?

Prayer Suggestion:

Open yourself to God's presence. Be aware of the pain Jesus must have experienced. Be aware of the pain and confusion and guilt the disciples must have felt. Bring to God whatever has surfaced in your own life and ask for God's healing touch, God's forgiving love.

Thursday, Fifth Week of Lent

Then the assembly rose as a body and brought Jesus before Pilate. They began to accuse him.... Then Pilate said to the chief priests and the crowds, "I find no basis for an accusation against this man." ... Pilate then called together the chief priests, the leaders, and the people, and said to them, "You brought me this man as one who was perverting the people; and here I have examined him in your presence and have not found this man guilty of any of your charges against him. Neither has Herod ... he has done nothing to deserve death. I will therefore have him flogged and release him."

Then they all shouted out together, "Away with this fellow! Release Barabbas for us!" ... They kept shouting, "Crucify, crucify him!" A third time he said to them, "... I have found in him no ground for the sentence of death; I will therefore have him flogged and then release him." But they kept urgently demanding with loud shouts that he should be crucified; and their voices prevailed. So Pilate gave his verdict that their demand should be granted.

—Luke 23:1-2a, 4, 13-18, 21-24

Pilate examined Jesus again and again and found no fault in him. Pilate sent Jesus to Herod because he belonged to Herod's jurisdiction, hoping Herod would make the hard decision. Luke tells us that Herod was glad to see Jesus; Herod had wanted to see Jesus for a long time and see some of the signs he had heard about. But Jesus said nothing when Herod questioned him and the chief priests and scribes continued vehemently accusing Jesus. So Herod and his soldiers joined the others, treating Jesus with contempt and mocking him. Then Herod passed the buck back to Pilate, finding no fault in him.

Pilate still found no fault in him, and tried to release him one more time. But the crowd was urgent and demanding and loud, and Pilate gave in.

It's hard to go against the crowd even when you know you are right; crowds are intimidating, frightening. It is hard to stand firm when everyone seems to be against you.

Have there been times when you went along with the crowd? How did you feel? Would you do something differently if you could do it over? What did you learn?

Have there been times when you did take a stand when most people disagreed with you? What were the circumstances? Who were the people involved?

How did you feel? What did you learn about taking risks? Write what comes.

Try to imagine the scenes described in the passage above. Where would you have been?

Prayer Suggestion:

Jesus knew what it felt like to have the majority against him. Offer to him those times you have failed. Ask for sensitivity to know when to take a stand and for courage to act when called to act.

To Walk With Jesus

Friday,
Fifth Week of Lent

Then the soldiers of the governor took Jesus into the
governor's headquarters, and they gathered the
whole cohort around him. They stripped him and
put a scarlet robe on him, and after twisting some
thorns into a crown, they put it on his head. They
put a reed in his right hand and knelt before him
and mocked him, saying, "Hail, King of the Jews!"
They spat on him, and took the reed and struck him
on the head. After mocking him, they stripped him
of the robe and put his own clothes on him. Then
they led him away to crucify him.

—Matthew 27:27-31

The sentence to crucify Jesus was not enough for the
angry, bloodthirsty crowd. They heaped jeers and mocking on top of the already heavy sentence. Jesus stood
before them all completely stripped, completely vulnerable. He was ridiculed, spat upon, mocked, beaten.
The crown of thorns weighed heavy on his brow. It
made no sense. His life had been one of healing and of
love. We want to ask why, but there is no answer. It only

shows us how far fear can take people and how strong love can be.

Have there been times in your life when you have felt vulnerable, exposed, stripped with no more masks to hide behind? What were the circumstances? What did you feel? Be as specific as you can.

Is this a memory that is still painful and in need of healing? If so, as you remember the time again, invite Jesus into the memory and listen for what he says to you. What does he do? What does he say? Record what comes.

When do you fear being vulnerable? What are the masks you hide behind? Which mask would you most fear removing?

Reread the story of Jesus' mocking. As you remember Jesus being stripped and mocked, what do you feel? Can you picture Jesus in this scene and give to him your most vulnerable moment? Can you remove any masks you may hide behind and talk to him just as you are? In your mind's eye, say to Jesus whatever you want to say. Listen for what he would say to you. Write whatever comes.

Prayer Suggestion:

It is difficult to be in pain and feel vulnerable, so we wear masks and build walls. But Jesus has been there before us. Be still in his presence and give him thanks for what he has already done in your life.

Saturday, Fifth Week of Lent

When they came to the place that is called The Skull,
they crucified Jesus there with the criminals, one on
his right and one on his left. Then Jesus said,
"Father, forgive them; for they do not know what
they are doing."

—Luke 23:33-34

The verdict was guilty. The sentence was crucifixion
and the angry mob was satisfied. Barabbas was set free.
Jesus dragged the heavy cross up Golgotha's hill. When
Jesus fell under the weight of the cross, Simon of Cyrene
was ordered to help Jesus carry his cross the rest of the
way. But no one could help Jesus when they reached the
top of the hill. The nails pounded through his flesh and
into the cross. The cross was raised. And Jesus hung
there alone, his life blood draining away.

Do you ever wonder where you would have been
that day? Hovering, cowering in the corner of some
courtyard? Trying to comfort another? Watching from
afar? Caught up in the cries of the crowd, "Crucify!
Crucify! Crucify!"? Casting lots at the foot of the cross?
Pounding in the nails? Weeping on Golgotha? Caught in
the agony of denial? Or maybe just running, running,

running? Replay the events in your mind. Where would you have been?

The events that happened that day were matters of life and death. And two thousand years later the questions are the same. We must decide where we are in relationship to the cross. It is difficult to be left untouched at the foot of the cross, to be neutral, for we must wrestle with the darkness of the cross if we would celebrate Easter morning. And as we wrestle with the darkness of the cross we must wrestle with the darkness of our own lives if we are to hear Jesus' words—words meant for us as surely as for those betrayers and executioners two thousand years ago—"Father, forgive them; for they do not know what they are doing."

Picture in your mind's eye Jesus on the cross. Sit at the foot of the cross for a while. Say whatever you would say. Be still and listen. Record whatever comes.

Prayer Suggestion:

Remain at the foot of the cross with Jesus. Listen for Jesus' words to you. Say to him whatever you want to say. Record whatever comes.

Review what you have done this week and record any additional insights that come.

Passion (or Palm) Sunday

Sixth Sunday of Lent

Lectionary readings from Year A:

Isaiah 50:4-7
Psalm 22
Philippians 2:6-11
Matthew 26:14—27:66

Lectionary readings from Year B:

Isaiah 50:4-7
Psalm 22
Philippians 2:6-11
Mark 14:1—15:47

Lectionary readings from Year C:

Isaiah 50:4-7
Psalm 22
Philippians 2:6-11
Luke 22:14—23:56

Each of the gospel readings for today is about Jesus' entry into Jerusalem. As you begin Holy Week you may want to spend a little extra time reading the entire passion story or the events of the last days of Jesus' life from one of the gospels. Some of those events have already been covered in the meditations; some will be covered during Holy Week. Little can take the place of choosing one of the gospels and prayerfully beginning Holy Week by entering Jerusalem with Jesus and continuing that walk with him through the resurrection. If you would like to take such a journey, read one of the following:

Matthew, chapters 21—28;

Mark, chapters 11—16;

Luke, chapters 19—24;

John, chapters 12—21.

Monday of Holy Week

Six days before the Passover Jesus came to Bethany, the home of Lazarus, whom he had raised from the dead. There they gave a dinner for him. Martha served, and Lazarus was one of those at the table with him. Mary took a pound of costly perfume made of pure nard, anointed Jesus' feet, and wiped them with her hair. The house was filled with the fragrance of the perfume.

—John 12:1-3

In John's gospel, the raising of Lazarus immediately precedes this event. The chief priests and Pharisees were frightened by the number of Jews now believing in Jesus, fearing the Romans would come to destroy them all. Orders were given for anyone who knew where Jesus was to report it so that he could be arrested.

It is not beyond belief that Mary knew of these orders and feared for Jesus' life and actually was anointing him as a prelude to coming events. But such reasoning is only conjecture, for the gospel writers do not tell us why Mary did what she did; they only tell us what she did. Anointing a special guest or beloved person was not unusual in an eastern home, but anointing the feet was reserved for burial. (Matthew and Mark say that the woman anointed Jesus' head.)

We know that Mary loved Jesus. Earlier she sat at his feet and listened to him while Martha prepared food for the guests; Jesus told her she had chosen wisely to be with him (Luke 10:38-42). Now he is in their home again after giving new life to her brother. She must have been overwhelmed with gratitude to Jesus.

It may be hard for us to enter the story and imagine what Mary felt. Our ways of expressing gratitude are different. Has there been a time when you have been overwhelmed with gratitude for something someone did for you? What did you do? Is there something you still need to do? How do you show love and gratitude? Record any memory that may surface.

The events that follow this anointing are the events that lead to Jesus' death. Spend some time now just being with Jesus as you would with a dear friend you knew was about to die. What do you feel? What do you say?

Prayer Suggestion:

Spend some time thumbing through one of the gospels. Give thanks for the events of Jesus' life, especially those events or those words that have special meaning for you now. Jot down the events or words of Jesus. Spend time with him in gratitude for whatever has surfaced.

Tuesday of Holy Week

When they had sung the hymn, they went out to the Mount of Olives. Then Jesus said to them, "You will all become deserters because of me this night." ... Peter said to him, "Though all become deserters because of you, I will never desert you." Jesus said to him, "Truly I tell you, this very night, before the cock crows, you will deny me three times." Peter said to him, "Even though I must die with you, I will not deny you." And so said all the disciples.

[After Jesus was arrested,] Peter was sitting outside in the courtyard. A servant-girl came to him and said, "You also were with Jesus the Galilean." But he denied it before all of them.... Another servant-girl saw him, and she said to the bystanders, "This man was with Jesus of Nazareth." Again he denied it with an oath, "I do not know the man." ... Bystanders came up and said to Peter, "Certainly you are also one of them, for your accent betrays you." Then he began to curse, and he swore an oath, "I do not know the man!" At that moment the cock crowed. Then Peter remembered what Jesus had said, "Before the cock crows, you will deny me three times." And he went out and wept bitterly.

—Matthew 26:30-35, 69-75

On the way to Gethsemane, Jesus told the disciples that they would all fall away from him. Those must have been hard words for the disciples to hear. Did Jesus not know how much they loved him? Peter protested, "I'll never fall away," and the other disciples echoed the same. "Before the cock crows," said Jesus. "Never," cried Peter. And Peter was soon asleep with the others in Gethsemane.

The rest happened so fast. Jesus was arrested and the disciples fled. Matthew tells us that Peter followed at a distance. Can you see him darting from tree to tree, trying to stay hidden in the shadows or milling in the courtyard with the crowd, straining to listen and trying to look inconspicuous?

But Peter's knees started knocking when a young maid observed, "You were with Jesus." "Not me!" cried Peter. Then a bystander made the same observation, and Peter denied it with an oath. Yet another bystander commented on Peter's accent, "His accent is like theirs!" And the strong, brave fisherman dissolved into a rage of oaths, silenced only by the crowing cock. The pain and the fears and the shame and the loss and the confusion dissolved into heaving sobs.

Peter's anguish becomes our own for every word we would take back, for every part of life we would erase but cannot. Can you identify with Peter? What were your circumstances? Make notes as you remember.

The pain of denial was great. Jesus loved Peter, and Peter came to know the depth of that love and the grace of forgiveness when Jesus appeared to him after the resurrection. Are there crevices inside you that still hold guilt and need to be brought into the light of Jesus' love and forgiveness?

Prayer Suggestion:

Ask God for the grace to receive forgiveness, and for the grace to forgive—even when it means forgiving yourself.

TO WALK WITH JESUS

Wednesday of Holy Week

While they were eating, Jesus took a loaf of bread, and after blessing it he broke it, gave it to the disciples, and said, "Take, eat; this is my body." Then he took a cup, and after giving thanks he gave it to them, saying, "Drink from it, all of you; for this is my blood of the covenant, which is poured out for many for the forgiveness of sins."

—Matthew 26:26-28

For I received from the Lord what I also handed on to you, that the Lord Jesus on the night when he was betrayed took a loaf of bread, and when he had given thanks, he broke it and said, "This is my body that is for you. Do this in remembrance of me." In the same way he took the cup also, after supper, saying, "This cup is the new covenant in my blood. Do this, as often as you drink it, in remembrance of me." For as often as you eat this bread and drink the cup, you proclaim the Lord's death until he comes.

—1 Corinthians 11:23-26

Nothing was the same about this night. Strange conversations filled the Passover meal, conversations about Jesus not eating or drinking with them again, about his body being broken. While they were celebrating in their customary way, giving thanks for the promises God had fulfilled in the old covenant, Jesus started talking about the blood of a new covenant. The dialogue at the table was disquieting and confusing, a conversation the disciples would only begin to understand days later.

Can you imagine what it might have been like to be there that night? Try to place yourself at the table that night and hear Jesus' words for the very first time. What do you feel? What do you do? What do you say to Jesus? What does he say to you?

Jesus' words to the disciples have become familiar words to us—words of forgiveness, words of promise of God's continued presence, words that connect us to Christ's body in the world. Sometimes words can become so familiar that we no longer hear them.

What do you think, what do you feel when you read these words again? What are your memories of the times and places and circumstances in which you have heard these words, received the bread and the cup in Jesus' name? What do you feel as you remember?

Are there particular times of celebrating the Lord's Supper that stand out to you? What was going on in your life?

TO WALK WITH JESUS

Jesus said that his body was broken for us—broken for our brokenness. His blood was shed for us—shed that we might have new life. What does this mean for you now, at this point in your Lenten journey?

Prayer Suggestion:

Be quiet in God's presence. Ask God to prepare you to receive all God has for you as you participate in this holy season again. Continue to meditate on Jesus' words as part of your preparation.

Maundy or Holy Thursday
(Thursday of Holy Week)

Now before the festival of the Passover, Jesus knew
that his hour had come to depart from this world
and go to the Father. Having loved his own who
were in the world, he loved them to the end. The
devil had already put it into the heart of Judas son of
Simon Iscariot to betray him. And during supper
Jesus … got up from the table, took off his outer
robe, and tied a towel around himself. Then he
poured water into a basin and began to wash the
disciples' feet and to wipe them with the towel that
was tied around him. He came to Simon Peter, who
said to him, "Lord, are you going to wash my feet?"
Jesus answered, "You do not know now what I am
doing, but later you will understand." Peter said to
him, "You will never wash my feet." Jesus
answered, "Unless I wash you, you have no share
with me."

After he had washed their feet, had put on his
robe, and had returned to the table, he said to them,
"Do you know what I have done to you? You call me
Teacher and Lord—and you are right, for that is
what I am. So if I, your Lord and Teacher, have

washed your feet, you also ought to wash one another's feet. For I have set you an example, that you also should do as I have done to you."

—John 13:1-8, 12-15

The roads in Palestine were deep in dust during the dry season and very muddy during the wet season. It was a common practice to have a water vessel at the door of a house and have a servant ready to wash the feet of guests. Guests would have bathed themselves before coming, so only the washing of the feet was necessary.

Jesus and his disciples had no servants, so in this last meal with them, Jesus took on the role of the servant. He did what no one else had thought to do.

Jesus sets the example of servanthood, and he emphasizes the importance of being cleansed by him—"Unless I wash you, you have no share with me." How do you think you would have responded to Jesus washing your feet? What would you have said? Felt? Done?

You have participated in many moments of self-examination this Lenten season. As you participate in the last days of Jesus' life on earth, is there any area you would like for him to cleanse now? Be specific. Write whatever comes.

After Jesus washed the disciples' feet, he put on his robe, returned to the table and said to them, "… So if I, your Lord and Teacher, have washed your feet, you also ought to wash one another's feet. For I have set you an example, that you also should do as I have done to you." How can we participate in the washing of another's feet? How might you participate in the cleansing process of another, in helping another experience acceptance as a child of God? Ask for God's insight in answering these questions and record whatever comes.

Prayer Suggestion:

Be still in Jesus' presence. Try to imagine yourself at that table that night. Offer to Jesus the part of you that you most want cleansed. Hear his words to you.

Good Friday
(Friday of Holy Week)

At three o'clock Jesus cried out with a loud voice, "Eloi, Eloi, lema sabachthani?" which means, "My God, my God, why have you forsaken me?"

—Mark 15:34

After this, when Jesus knew that all was now finished, he said (in order to fulfill the scripture), "I am thirsty." … When Jesus had received the wine, he said, "It is finished." Then he bowed his head and gave up his spirit.

—John 19:28, 30

It was now about noon, and darkness came over the whole land until three in the afternoon, while the sun's light failed; and the curtain of the temple was torn in two. Then Jesus, crying with a loud voice, said, "Father, into your hands I commend my spirit." Having said this, he breathed his last.

—Luke 23:44-46

As far as the disciples could see, the crucifixion was un-conditional defeat. Their hope of a new life, a new kingdom, hung nailed to a cross. The darkness was pierced by Jesus' anguished cry, "My God, my God, why have you forsaken me?" Everything seemed as bleak, desolate, and dark as the surrounding sky. The whole universe seemed to be weeping. Can you imagine what those scattered disciples must have been feeling?

Can you imagine yourself at the foot of the cross, or maybe hiding somewhere in the crowd as Jesus breathed his last breath?

Stay with that image for a few minutes. What do you feel? What do you do?

We know the rest of the story. In what seemed to be the bleakest hour of history, there is hope. Jesus took a deep breath and breathed his last. But Jesus' final cry, "It is finished!" was not a cry of despair, but of completion, victory, fulfillment, relief. Jesus' job was finished. God's love was unleashed as those outstretched arms shouted once and for all that forgiveness still follows failure, life still follows death, hope still follows defeat.

Without death there is no resurrection. Early in this Lenten journey you reflected on what you wanted to give up or what part of you must die so that you might experience new life. As you reflect on your Lenten journey now, what do Jesus' words, "It is finished" mean to you? Be specific. Write whatever comes.

As you continue to meditate on Jesus' crucifixion, read the story of the crucifixion again from one or more of the gospels: Matthew 27:32-54, Mark 15:20-39, Luke 23:26-49, and John 19:16-37.

Prayer Suggestion:

Be still in God's presence as you wait at the foot of the cross.

Easter Vigil
(Saturday of Holy Week)

When it was evening, there came a rich man from
Arimathea, named Joseph, who was also a disciple
of Jesus. He went to Pilate and asked for the body of
Jesus; then Pilate ordered it to be given to him. So
Joseph took the body and wrapped it in a clean linen
cloth and laid it in his own new tomb, which he had
hewn in the rock. He then rolled a great stone to the
door of the tomb and went away.

—Matthew 27:57-60

But those who wait for the LORD
    shall renew their strength,
  they shall mount up with wings
    like eagles,
they shall run and not be weary,
  they shall walk and not faint.

—Isaiah 40:31

Jesus was laid in the tomb. The tomb was sealed. It
seemed like the end—so final. That in-between time,
from the sealing of the tomb until Easter morning,
spanned an eternity.

To Walk With Jesus

And so it seems with our waiting. Life is filled with waiting. Waiting. Wondering. Asking why. Grieving losses. Hoping. And waiting again.

Only as we begin to glimpse the sunrise, catch that first ray of light, can we begin to understand what the waiting has been about. And even then the dawn sometimes seems to come slowly, for our eyes are not yet fully open. What have been significant times of waiting in your life? How did dawn come?

How have your times of waiting been like the waiting the disciples must have experienced after the tomb was sealed?

As we wait in this Easter Vigil, review where you have been on this journey through Lent. As you come to the end of your Lenten journey, can you embrace God's promise, "Those who wait for the LORD shall renew their strength, they shall mount up with wings like eagles, they shall run and not be weary, they shall walk and not faint"? What does this promise mean to you now?

As you continue your Easter Vigil, you may want to read some or all of the following passages that recount the whole of salvation history: Genesis 1:1—2:2; Psalm 104; Genesis 22:1-18; Psalm 16; Exodus 14:15—15:18; Isaiah 54:5-14; Psalm 30; Isaiah 55:1-11; Isaiah 12:2-6; Baruch 3:9-15, 32—4:4; Psalm 19; Ezekiel 36:16-28; Psalm

42; Romans 6:3-11; Psalm 118; Matthew 28:1-10; Mark 16:1-8; Luke 24:1-12.

Write any reflections that come.

Prayer Suggestion:

Prayerfully read back through what has surfaced during these forty days and give thanks to God for God's presence with you throughout your journey. Rest in God's presence as you wait for new life to dawn.

Easter Sunday

The Resurrection of the Lord

Lectionary readings for Years A, B, and C:
      Acts 10:34a, 37-43
      Psalm 118
      Colossians 3:1-4 or 1 Corinthians 5:6b-8
      John 20:1-9

He is risen! Alleluia!

Read the Easter gospel passage now, joining with Mary Magdalene, Peter, and John as they go to visit the tomb. Weep with Mary at the tomb. Linger with her in the garden. As Jesus calls Mary's name, can you hear him calling your name, too? Will you recognize and believe in him?

On this Easter Sunday, you may want to prepare yourself for the renewal of your baptismal vows, joining with the body of believers with whom you worship. If there is no such service planned in your area you may prayerfully reaffirm what you have come to believe using your own words or the following Renewal of Baptismal Vows.

Renewal of Baptismal Vows

I once again reject sin and renounce evil
and its power in the world.
I renounce the ways of sin that separate
me from the love of God.
I turn again to Jesus Christ and accept
him as my Lord and Savior.
I intend to be Christ's faithful disciple,
obeying his word, and showing his love,
to my life's end.
I affirm my belief that the grace of God,
the presence of the living Christ, and
the empowerment of the Holy Spirit
are with me in this moment and
will be with me all my life long.
Amen.

Prayer Suggestion:

Go forth this day rejoicing, allowing each
breath you breathe to be a prayer of thanksgiving
for new life.

Morning has broken! The dawn has come! The tomb
is empty! He has risen! Alleluia! Amen!